For the Love of Nine Muses

Eddie Morales

For the Love of Nine Muses

Copyright © 2015 by Eddie Morales

www.poeticon.com

All rights reserved. No part of this book may be reproduced or transmitted in any form or by any means without written permission of the author.

ISBN 9781938094057

DEDICATED

TO ALL WHO HAVE

LOVED AND LOST AND LOVED

AND LOST AND SO ON

Table of Contents

FIONA 11

    So It Began 13

    A Cold Ocean 14

    Silent Courtship 16

    Brimstone in the Fire 18

    Zipped Up 20

    Rewind 22

    Our First Kiss 24

    Love Poem for Fiona 26

    A New Moon 27

    A Parting Kiss 29

ISAVELLA 31

    Bigger Dreams 33

    The Art of Woo War 35

    All is Not Fair in Woo and War 37

    Bar Magnet 38

    No Apple for this Adam 40

    Who is Courting Whom? 42

    The Promise of Carnal Knowledge 44

    Movie Sequel 47

Decision Split 49

Deceptive Ending 51

BESSA MAE 53

The Dance 55

Making Gray 57

Lifetime of Love in Four Hours 59

Love on the Phone 61

The Confrontation 63

We Dance Again 65

Home Sour Sweet Home 68

The Expectant Letter 70

Saved by a Letter 72

The End of Summer 74

RAVENETTE 75

Visiting Aguada 77

The Swimming Hole 79

Fire and Fury 81

Moody 83

Distress Signal 85

NYC Rendezvous 87

Foreboding 88

Hospital Stay 89

Letter to an Angel 90

Grave Goodbye 91

JAMEENA 93

Jameena's Exotic Dance 95

The Lure 96

A Face in the Crowd 97

In a Far Away Place 99

The Rape of Jameena 100

Café au Lait 101

Sweet Chocolate 102

Blending In 103

Onstage Looking Out 104

Chicago Bound 105

AKSHARANI 107

Unexpected Guest 109

Exoticness 111

Satisfying Hunger 112

Paradise 113

Repartee 115

For a Pink Lotus 116

The Noiseless Deity 119

The Arrow of Love 120

One for Tradition 121

A Wedding 122

YU-SEONG 123

The Introduction 125

Moon in the Flesh 126

No Shame 127

Selfish 128

Days of Blue 129

Foolishness 130

Petals 131

Yet Another Fleeting Moment 132

An Understanding 133

Not in the Stars 134

BAYBEE 135

Bodacious Baybee..137

No Venus 138

I Don't Blame the Wind 139

Savage Love 140

String Haiku for my Baybee 141

Take Your Time 142

Brief Encounter 143

The Bed 144

Flowers Bloom 145

Meteoric 146

ESPERANZA 147

Hope 149

About the Author 151

FIONA

SO IT BEGAN

Fiona
My friend,
Since time memory served,
One day,
By Nature's grace,
Transformed my eyes.

Her face glowed
Surpassing daylight.

Her pink blouse failed
In its task of concealment
Where rosebuds overwhelmed
Her tomboyish charm.

Her black hair
Almost hip length
Caressed her face.

Her eyes
Obsidian beacons
Secretly provided
My mind with daring scenarios.
Afterwards
That night
In the total darkness of my bedroom
Her face hung on my ceiling . . .
A full moon.

A COLD OCEAN

Fiona and I went to the beach
Like many times before,
And the sun was hot,
But tepid upon my skin.

Even silently walking
Next to her had the makings
Of an awkward moment,
And I was losing my mind.

Where on the sandy strip
Was I going to hide?

The beach was packed.

Everyone would notice the power
Of the caterpillar's metamorphosis.

We stopped for a moment.
She asked me:

"What do you want to do?"
(Kiss you, I thought)

A few moments passed before
I realized we were gazing at each other,
Not saying a word,
Her snug pink bathing suit
Silently speaking on her behalf,
Whether she knew it or not,

And I panicked—
And I blurted out:

    "Last one in the water loses!"

Then I ran towards the ocean,

With Fiona close behind me,

Laughing like the little girl,

And I dove into the freezing Atlantic.

It was the only natural force on Earth

Cold and deep enough to stop a butterfly.

SILENT COURTSHIP

I go and pick Fiona up at her house—

Her dad approves of me,

And her mom definitely approves.

How lucky can I get?

We leave for a nice night out.

It's dark in the movie theater

We sit in the balcony way in the back

We hold hands

We whisper sweet nothings to each other

My arm moves over her shoulder

My hand finds comfort on one of her breasts

Her hand slides across my thigh

And touches me.

It's *very* dark in the balcony.

Our heads lean against each other

Her breathing is hot and heavy against my neck

I blow my hot breath against her earlobe

I nibble on her earlobe,

Earring and all.

It is *pitch* black in the balcony.

We do wonderful things to each other.

We miss the whole movie because of it.

The evening could've gone that way,

But first things first—

I wondered:

Would she consent to be my girlfriend?

BRIMSTONE IN THE FIRE

What a big difference from the movie theater,

Sitting in Saint Anthony's next to Fiona.

Our parents did this every Sunday,

For our own good.

There was too much lighting and I felt exposed.

I knew I was going to Hell for sure,

And Fiona would go to Heaven, and I'd never

See her again for all eternity.

(After all, it was *my* movie scenario, not hers)

And what about what Father Steltz

Said to me in his sermon?

> You must remain pure of body!
>
> You must be pure of thought!
>
> You must have a pure heart!
>
> You must be pure for this, and pure for that!
>
> Or you will *burn* for this, and *burn* for that!
>
> And while you're at it, you'll *burn* some more!

What a wonderful and merciful God.

Still too much lighting and I felt exposed.

Also, one must not covet.
Knowing what that meant,
I still did that at the movies.

And one must not lie.
I failed that one the day
Before at confession.
No way was I going to tell
Father Steltz the truth.
So I confessed to some nicer sins.

Why is an hour at the movies too short,
While an hour in church is too long?
Didn't matter, I was going to Hell anyway.

ZIPPED UP

I worked up the courage to ask Fiona out.
It was no easy task, even though I had done so
Many times in my mind,
And her answer was always yes.

It was a different thing to do so in person.

My heart was pounding, my palms were sweaty,
I kept forgetting the lines I had rehearsed every
Night for days while lying awake in bed, gazing at
Fiona's face as it covered the whole of my ceiling.
Awake because I feared she might say no.

I heard one could go blind from self-manipulation,
But who can blame a young man when he can't
Get the girl of his dreams out of his head.

I waited outside for her,
Near the school's front entrance,
Until she finally came out.

It was time to make my move,

So I called out her name, and she turned

To look at me.

I stared at her, the Medusa-like

Effect of her beautiful face

Turning me into marble from head to toe.

My lips zipped up, I froze,

Except my heart was still pounding on the inside.

    "See you tomorrow,"

Was all I said.

REWIND

I saw Fiona talking to some guy one morning.

My heart stopped and I couldn't breathe.

After that, I knew I couldn't take any more chances.

That Sunday, after church,

I finally asked her out.

But I didn't go empty handed—

I wrote her a poem.

I didn't care if it was a corny one.

I was afraid of *no*, but I had to find out,

So I read her the poem,

Then I quoted Shakespeare:

> So long as men can breathe, or eyes can see,
>
> So long lives this, and this gives life to thee.

(It went well with the *thou* and *thee* of church)

I had looked up Shakespeare at the library.

Didn't understand him much,

But those words stuck out for some reason.

Then I just flat out said: Wanna be my girlfriend?

Her lovely eyes Medusa-froze me

While I waited for her answer . . .

Then I melted five seconds later when she finally said:

    "Okay."

An eternity had passed in those five seconds.

OUR FIRST KISS

Our families got together at our house for dinner.
Afterwards, the grownups went to the living room,
To talk and watch television.

Fiona and I, and her sisters, and my sisters,
Stayed in the dining room, having dessert.
All done, the others took the dishes to the kitchen,
And we found ourselves alone.

The light to the dining room was turned off,
So we stood out of everyone's sight.
We didn't even speak.
I couldn't speak

I felt the butterflies tap dancing on my stomach floor.
Still, some natural attraction brought us together.

I leaned over and kissed her,
Her lips, so soft and tender,
And I remember she kissed me back.

Then, there was mayhem in the living room.

"Fionaaaaaaaaaa!" Her sisters screamed.
"Come! You're going to miss it!"

The television volume rose, and I heard:
"She loves you, yeah, yeah, yeah!"

Those damn Beatles!

I remember Fiona dashing to the living room
And going nuts at the same time.

And I recall saying to Paul McCartney under my breath:
I think she loves *you* even more.

LOVE POEM FOR FIONA

I wrote another love poem for Fiona.
In it I told her I would woo her
Underneath the stars
With the silver moon staring down at us,
Illuminating our bodies in the darkness,
Our bodies tangled up in each other
Like the roots of a tree,
Or our torsos flat against each other,
With our arms and legs for tree limbs.

Me tasting like vanilla
Which she loved
Fiona tasting like chocolate
Which I loved.

I said I'd put two drops of vanilla on my tongue
And kiss her the way they kiss in Paris.
Afterwards, we sleep in each other's arms,
Wake up the following morning to greet the sun,
And show the sun how we kissed in front of the moon.

Well, after reading the poem, Fiona said
She read the same magazine, and
Nice girls don't do those kind of things.
Then she streaked away.

Huh?
What magazine?
Nice girls don't what?
Damn.

A NEW MOON

My sister gave me the bad news—
Fiona's family was moving away.
Far away.
Impossibly far away.
Another continent far away.
Beyond the moon far away.
Across the galaxy far away.

I walked around with a giant stone in my stomach,
And all that was left to do was jump in the ocean.

I'd sink, like my heart sank,
Not having talked to her enough,
Not having gone for enough walks,
Not having hugged her enough,
Not having kissed her enough.
Having kissed her only once.

Only once.
Damn! Only once.

Mercy is sure God's way.
I was sure God would send me to
Hell for a good reason.

And I figured there was no use in crying

Since Shakespeare would have said

We were condemned to part.

But what's so sweet about it?

In bed that night,

I saw what the other side

Of the silver moon looked like—

A blackout.

A PARTING KISS

Of all things!
A quick hug,
And a peck on the cheek.
(Not at all the way Parisians kiss)

What else were Fiona and I supposed to do?
Our two families were all there,
No one knew we were going out,
And I'm not sure I knew either.

Parting and sorrow.
Sorrow and parting.
I told Shakespeare to shut up!
Was he blind?
It was the end of the world!

Anyhow, after their car sped around the corner,
My mom put her arms around me,
Hugged me, and whispered:
"There's a cute girl moving in across the street."
Then she went inside.

Mom didn't realize what I had to go through in life.
The agony, the sadness
And the turmoil of a dying heart.
Jeepers! It was the end of my world!
And all she could say . . .
Wait, I thought.
What cute girl?

ISAVELLA

BIGGER DREAMS

Turns out the girl across the street,

Isavella, was cute alright, like my Mom said.

Damn cute! Precociously cute!

Tall, slim, and anatomically uplifting.

Doll Barbie probably went flat-chested with envy.

WOW!

Now, what to do?

In my head was a first-year college brain

In a ninth-grader's body.

Also, I was cursed, having the nickname *Bookworm*

Since cute girls didn't go out with bookworms,

But a blessing her brother, Pablo, wound up in my class.

We hit it off, I not caring he was in the ninth grade

With an eighth-grader's brain. Still, a nice, decent pal.

From that day onward, Pablo and I hung out all the time.

Then one day Pablo invited me to his house.

I met his mom and dad, his brother,

And four sisters, especially Isavella.

WOW!

I presented myself like a decent young man,

And Isavella presented me with ample cleavage.

I wondered if her parents

Would let me take her to the movies.

Of course, I was hoping to have

My hands full with all of her love.

THE ART OF WOO WAR

Isavella was taller than me,
By a couple of inches,
And her mom was even taller.

For some reason, the two of them
Reminded me of something
I read about the Black Widow Spider.
Anyway, whatever it was
It would come to me.

All I knew was—
I was dying to be alone with Isavella.
And we were, for a few minutes,
While Pablo was looking
For his baseball in his tornado-hit bedroom.
Her other siblings had gone outside,
And luckily her mom and dad were working.

I had learned a lesson about not being shy,
So, I quickly asked her if she would be my girlfriend,
And before I could blink, she said: "Yes!"
That was yes with an exclamation point for sure.

After a blink, her arms shot out,
Grabbed me tightly,
And I thought I was going to
Have to swallow her tongue
In order to breathe again.

(Eat your hearts out Parisians!)

Then we heard Pablo yell out he found the baseball.

Isavella *sprang* back as if nothing had happened.

Right then and there it came to me.

Black Widow Spiders are pretty fast.

ALL IS NOT FAIR IN WOO AND WAR

Isavella's mom went with us to the movies.
It was that or no go.
Plus we had to sit lower level,
And a decent distance from the screen,
Which meant too much light.
Isavella to my right,
Her mom to my left.
Ouch.

It could've been worse.
Her mom could've sat between us.

So, I had to keep my hands respectable.
Isavella's Maidenform Bra would
Have to hold onto them for me.

And Isavella,
Poor Isavella,
Hungry Isavella,
Had to purse her lips.

No French kissing *that* night.
All flights to Paris had been canceled.
So, we had to settle for a
Benedictine monastery in Italy.

BAR MAGNET

Isavella and her mom,
If placed feet to feet,
Would've made a bar magnet.

If her mom said something positive,
Isavella would say something negative.

If her mom said something negative,
Isavella would counter.

Then it got better.

If her mom agreed with me,
Isavella would disagree.
If her mom disagreed with me,
Isavella would take my side.

If you put their heads together,
You'd think they would stick,

One being positive and the other negative,

Opposites attracting and all that.

Well, that was a negative.

So, what was the positive?

I was positively sure I was the paperclip.

NO APPLE FOR THIS ADAM

I imagined a treeless Garden of Eden.

I imagined Isavella and me in that garden, naked.

Natural beauty that is innocence

Cannot walk in better beauty

But it walk in the best of beauty—

Nude.

Which is better?

Nude or naked?

It all depends.

If I conjure up Isavella's mom

As the serpent, there's no harm to be had.

This serpent seeks to bite me surely,

In this scenario, for what is on my mind.

Naked for sure will bring the bite.

Isavella remains the innocent, thereby nude.

However, in my nakedness, I too am innocent,

For *this* serpent dare not speak of any knowledge,

Because there is no tree.

I wished the serpent would go away

So I could plant a tree.

That's what I should've done first in my garden.

Then we *all* would've been naked.

WHO IS COURTING WHOM?

The flu is no fun, and bedridden Isavella had it,
Which kept me in conversation with her mother,
And nothing was certain but the feeling I had,
Of telepathic thoughts of Paris.

It was the motherly hugs,
A second or two too long.
The insistence on having me
Sit next to her on the sofa.

Isavella's dad worked two jobs,
And maybe mom just needed someone to talk to.

So we talked,
And talked,
And talked some more.

In a moment of laughter she squeezed my knee.
(Nothing to think about)

Then we told more jokes and laughed,

And the squeezing went higher,

By quick degrees.

(Something to think about)

(Danger, Will Robinson!)

Then our eyes met in a most awkward moment of silence.

(Time to leave)

On my way home, the little devil on my shoulder said:

    "You should've squeezed her back."

I agreed, and the little angel said:

"Stop it! Both of you!"

THE PROMISE OF CARNAL KNOWLEDGE

One day, mid-winter,

Isavella and I skipped school.

We were going to do it.

One of my friends offered me his place

Since his mom and dad were away.

It was going to be heaven!

I took some poems with me,

Love poems by famous poets,

Even though I knew she wouldn't understand them.

She'd rather kiss anyway.

And we did.

I fumbled with her sweater,

But she'd rather kiss instead.

The second sweater was a bit much I thought,

But she wanted to kiss instead.

The third sweater came off,

And we kissed some more.

Then the blouse came off,

And she said that's it for the tops for the moment.

Her skirt's removal,

And that of her three slips,

Bared three pairs of hose.

Waist high.

I helped remove the first layer,

Then the second layer,

Then finally, the third.

And she said that's it for the bottom for the moment.

It would've been easier to peel an onion.

Then she said, "Oh, Oh."

I said, "No."

She said, "Yes."

I said, "Oh no."

She replied, "Oh yes."

I said, "No, no, no."

She said, "Yes, yes, yes."

"Are you sure?" I asked.

"I'm positive!" Isavella shot back.

"It's my time of the month."

And that was the end of that—

Period!

MOVIE SEQUEL

Martial arts movie: *The Silver Fox.*

Lily Ho plays awesome swordswoman Ching Ching.

We're way back in the balcony.

Pablo to my left, his girl, Gina, to *his* left.

Isavella to my right.

No moms or dads.

It's dark.

The girls wanted to smooch.

Perfect!

Movie Starts.

Best fight movie ever!

Pow! Clang! Crunch! Boom! Ka-pow!

Amazing!

Ting! Ping! Pang! Tonk! Tank! Thunk!

Pablo and I are going nuts!

Swoosh! Squish! Squash! Ta-dunk!

Swords everywhere,

Punches everywhere,

Kicks everywhere,

And Pablo and I are going even more nuts!

Movie over. WOW! Lights come on.

I ask Pablo, "Hey, where's your girlfriend, Gina?"

Pablo replies, "I don't know. Where's Isavella?"

I reply, "I don't know, but hey, should we watch it again?"

Dumb question.

DECISION SPLIT

I got the scholarship.

Private high school.

I would have to go to summer school

At Williams College, some place in

Massachusetts.

Isavella was happy,

And not happy.

I was ecstatic.

I don't believe there's ever been

A reverse metamorphosis of a butterfly,

Unless you consider death.

We were too young for Death.

Isavella's attentions were stronger,

And her kisses more urgent,

Where sugar soured compared to them.

One last night in Paris hurt like hell in my heart,

And I swear I thought I

Heard Shakespeare laughing.

DECEPTIVE ENDING

Turns out Isavella was not a
Black Widow Spider after all,
Or she would have killed me
Instead of letting go of me.

It seems I escaped her mom too,
For different reasons.

(Isavella's dad found out her
Mom was cheating on him
And he almost killed her)

The lover almost kills the Widow,
That's a switch.
Practically overnight Isavella and
Her family moved out and that was that.

Nero of Rome must have had a twin brother in Paris,
Since the fires couldn't be put out.

BESSA MAE

THE DANCE

Summer, 1968
Scene I

In the beginning all is innocent.
Williams College,
Host to Mount Holyoke.

Scholarship boys meet
Scholarship girls for a dance.

Chaperones everywhere.

What was I doing? I wanted to go home.
Seemed everyone was paired up except
Me and a couple of my new friends.

Suddenly, I saw a nice looking figure go by,
Left to right, then, right to left.
The dim lighting off her light blue dress
Also went left, right, left, right.
She appeared to be looking for someone,
Or trying to get noticed, and if so, I noticed.

As I approached her, I got a good look at her face.
I didn't know angels came in black.
I asked her if she would like to dance.
She stared at me, surprised, perhaps shocked.
We exchanged names, and she looked around to
See if anyone was watching us.

Still, Bessa Mae, with a brilliant smile said,
    "I'd love to."
Her name, Bessa Mae, I told her, reminded me of a
Spanish song my mother often sang, *Bésame Mucho.*
I told her *Bésame* means *kiss me,* and that I liked that.

Or was it, "I'd like that."
I prefer remembering it as the latter.

MAKING GRAY

Summer, 1968

Scene II

People were staring, and I wondered why.
Didn't care.

The Temptations played on with *My Girl*.
I was a NYC boy slow-dancing with a
Baltimore girl.
Spanish Harlem acknowledging
Harlem Black was all.
Nothing wrong with that in my book.
And Bessa Mae was a bookworm like me.
What could be better?

I recited lines from
Farewell from Welfare Island
By Julia de Burgos,
She gave me Claude McKay's *Harlem Dancer*.

I gave her Lope de Vega's *Dulce Desdén*,

She gave me Langston Hughes.

Those were some sad lines from Langston:

> . . .
>
> *Says if you was to ask me*
>
> *How de blues they come to be—*
>
> *You wouldn't need to ask me:*
>
> *Just look at me and see!*

For three hours we danced, and talked,

And kissed, and tried to make gray

Out of black and white.

LIFETIME OF LOVE IN FOUR HOURS

Summer, 1968

Scene III

The first hour of the dance we fell in love.
The second hour we got to know each other.
The third hour of the dance we knew we were
Meant for each other, and we needed each other.
The remaining hour was agony, knowing we
Would be heading back to our respective lives.
|
I walked Bessa Mae back to her waiting bus,
Stopping to kiss her every minute or so,
Desperately hoping for some delay that
Would keep us together a little longer.

We ignored the faces of shock all
Around us, faces frozen as if some law had
Been broken, as if we had done something taboo.
So, I recited this poem of mine to her:

Love is love, and when we close our eyes,

We feel love, smell love, hear love,

And taste love; and when we open our

Eyes, what matters is that we see love,

Colorless and colorful.

We made promises to call and write.
Then Bessa Mae, crying, pulled away,
Boarded the bus, and the bus took her from me.
That night, together, Langston and I sang the blues;
And the way I felt, I knew how the Blues came to be.

LOVE ON THE PHONE

Summer, 1968

Scene IV

From Mount Holyoke,

To Williams College,

It was love calling me on the phone,

Love with the name Bessa Mae.

A ten-minute call limit, and she called *me*.

We must've ached more than we talked,

Because I don't remember what we said;

But I remember the agonizing space between us.

We could've been a hair-thickness away

From each other, and it would've still been too far.

We figured it was over, no denying it.

Still, we made plans to find each other somehow.

Just in case Romeo and Juliet survived the tragedy.

Time flew by like a meteor.

It was now my turn for a call.

I called her back so we could be blue

Together for another ten minutes.

THE CONFRONTATION

Summer, 1968

Scene V

After the phone call to Bessa Mae,
One of the three said,
"What the hell do you think you're doing?"
The second of the three said,
"We saw you at the dance. Stick to your own kind."

Such wrathful voices with livid eyes.
Filled with a hatred of the past,
A past rooted in the South.

I figured April 4th was still fresh on their minds,
But I had nothing to do with that.
My people didn't shoot Martin Luther King, Jr.

Luckily, one of the black proctors happened by,
And probably saved me from a beating.

My kind.

Quite a sobering thought,

To be light of skin,

And not wanted by the blacks,

And . . .

Not wanted by the whites.

My kind.

Good thing Bessa Mae and I

Were of the human kind.

WE DANCE AGAIN

Summer, 1968

Scene VI

The turning point.
Another dance,
Mount Holyoke College
Hosts Williams College.
It was an answered prayer.

When all is against life,
Life finds a way,
And as long as life continues,
Love will find a way.
It is the only way the stars
Can become uncrossed,
Thereby, allowing Romeo and Juliet to survive.

Bessa Mae and I survived.
Therefore, we danced, but it was not enough.

So,

Swiftly thwarted were the chaperones.

We fled into the summer night,

Which was far too swiftly in our heated favor,

With its balmy air,

And its zephyr stalking us through the trees,

Just cool enough to fan the flame,

But not enough to douse it,

And a silver moon to serve as witness,

And swelled up full to serve up madness.

Fire burns and burn it did,

With the fiercest fire of all youth,

And Virginity gave her life for love.

Then the sirens of the chaperones called out.

One was missing, and the bus detained.

The hours had fled and the footrace was on.

I was late, but accounted for.

With no time left for goodbyes,

I sadly waved my madness away.

"Bésame," I yelled out of the window, "I'll write you."

On the ride back to Williams College, I wondered

Which was worse, dying like Romeo and Juliet,

Or parting never to see each other again.

I'd think about it later.

At that moment, I just wanted to figure out

How to get to her house in Baltimore.

HOME SOUR SWEET HOME

Summer, 1968

Scene VII

Summer was not over but it was over.

Williamstown and Mount Holyoke,

Two cities on the other side of the foggy

Window of my mind had become a mystery.

It was a surrealistic play, and

The characters had vanished.

Would there be a revival?

No.

The play was over.

The mid-summer night's dream was a balloon.

The needle of reality sharp.

Others would be there to blow up their own balloons.

Life had suddenly become serious

On my side of the window.

The only thing clear was Bessa Mae.

We wrote each other a letter

As soon as we got home.

I sent her my photo, she sent me hers,

First chance we got.

Whether Williamstown to NYC or

Mount Holyoke to Baltimore,

The distance to the moon remained the same.

THE EXPECTANT LETTER

Summer, 1968

Scene VIII

I received her letter.

Bessa Mae was afraid.

The Cycle of Life cannot

Continue unless the cycle is broken,

In this case, possibly for nine months or so.

Then both cycles continue.

We were an oxymoron for sure:

>*Dumb Bookworms.*

I *was* dumbstruck.

Mixed feelings.

Was this good or was this bad?

Life is good, but this was bad, bad, bad.

Statistically speaking.

Something involving shotguns.

Something about a wise man becoming a fool.

What about teenagers?

Even smart ones.

What do they become?

The answer stared me in the face.

Take away the "oxy."

SAVED BY A LETTER

Summer, 1968

Scene IX

I received a second letter.
Bessa Mae was in the red.
False alarm. Better late
If her cycle is not on time.

Mixed feelings again.
Was this good or was this bad?
Life is good, no doubt, but this was better.

Life barely lived is barely life at all.
Yet often Youth does find a way to cross two stars.
Bessa Mae and I were almost crossed as well.

I secretly called her, hoping she would be
The one to pick up the phone.
I'd hang up if she didn't.

Bessa Mae answered, unbelievably.

She as well had secretly planned to call me.

We talked, were relieved, and we agreed.

We were too young for a shotgun wedding.

THE END OF SUMMER

Summer, 1968
Scene X

The denouement.
Autumn, the killer of summer,
Entered from the wing, and summer died.
By slow degrees.
My letters traveled quickly, but
Bessa Mae and the moon
Had become equidistant.

It was a dream.
A wonderful, glorious dream,
Born in the middle of summer,
On crazy nights,
During moments of freedom,
When crazy things are supposed to happen.
Wonderful things as well as dangerous ones.
One last phone call said it all.
(I wish you well)
Even parents say the same thing.

I realized to be true:

Parents cannot protect you forever.
That would be a jail sentence.

RAVENETTE

VISITING AGUADA

July, my seventeenth birthday.

Midnight.

Brightest moon.

I am in the birthplace of my parents.

I was born the next town north, Aguadilla,

On an army cot because there were no beds

Available at that hospital.

So my mother said.

Then to NYC six months later.

Now I was back for a visit with my dad.

It is where I met her.

Pelo de cuervo (hair of raven) they called her.

I called her Ravenette,

After Poe's obsession.

Her eyes, being of age,

Promised fire, and her body left

No doubt it could keep that promise.

We asked each other so many irrelevant

Questions for the sake of those around us,

Until everyone else went home or to bed.

Ravenette and I were wide-awake,

The fire in her eyes more evident,

And from motionless, as if some danger lurked

Nearby, she suddenly came to life,

Catching me unprepared.

"Enough of this," she said. "Make love to me already!"

She got no argument from me.

THE SWIMMING HOLE

El Salto they called it.
The Jump because tree branches
Hung out low and far enough over the water
To use as diving boards.
After a heavy rain was the best time.

Ravenette wore a red one-piece bathing suit
Underneath an open pink shirt,
Tied at the waist, and a lime cotton skirt.
Brilliant colors fighting her black mane.
She took the pink and lime off in preparation.

I jumped first, surfaced, and searched for her.

Red and black pierced the bright yellow sun,
On a branch, balanced, poised, like a statue.

Magnificent!
As if with wings, airborne,

Defying gravity, aloft for several minutes,

I expected her to alight on the surface

And walk nimbly upon the water.

Good thing she plunged into the fluid net,

Because angels can't make love.

FIRE AND FURY

Ravenette had more than fire for love.
She could also hate with equal detonation.

No one challenged her when she raged.
I couldn't; I did not really know her.
The aftermath of her fury, though, proved intoxicating.

It was the sneaking out of her window.
Late that night.

It was the tapping on my window,
A tapping with a hint of a threat if I did not open.

It was the pouncing agility of her body,
And the overhead fan blowing her heat over me.

The way she locked her lips over my mouth to quiet me.
And it was the chill down my spine
At the thought of discovery by my relatives

That made my heart race and my body betray me.

And the force with which she claimed me,

Which made me crave her so,

Even if I were told I'd die thereafter.

MOODY

The sun was beating us,

Even in the shade, and

Too tiring for

Conversation.

I observed,

Perplexed,

Trying to figure out

Ravenette's pacifier.

She wore nothing else.

No way to kiss her.

Not on the lips anyway.

Too hot to kiss anyway.

Any way too hot for other things.

Then movement.

Slow, serpentine stretching across one side

Of the bed, then slowly to the other side.

Finally, one leg parted from the other,

Which I would have taken as an invitation,

And the leg sneaked slowly over the edge, then

Her body followed in a heat-drunken stupor.

Beads of sweat trickled down her back,

While her lazy wave begged me to follow,

While her slow-motion hips

Led the way to the shower.

There under the cool water we embraced,

Without scalding each other;

And I did nothing but listen to

Ravenette nurse on her pacifier.

DISTRESS SIGNAL

Wild things create danger

Whether prey or predator.

I know,

I was devoured—

Completely.

I created the danger by being there

For her to devour me,

Over and over again.

Not once did I flee.

Ravenette created the danger

Because she was there,

And she had to do what she had to do.

Now I had to fly from San Juan to NYC,

And Ravenette pled with me to

Take her with me.

I couldn't, not because I didn't want to,

But because Fate had chewed and spit us out

Into different worlds.

NYC RENDEZVOUS

Ravenette found me.
Accidentally?
Did Fate have second thoughts?
Could be.

Her Raven's hair looked a little dull,
And her face and figure a little thinner.
We got together, to rekindle
And old flame.
Try, anyway.
Something was not right, going through the motions.
I used every precaution, just in case,
More for my protection than hers.

And I had a curious thought—
A de-clawed and toothless
Cat is useless on the hunt.
I missed the teeth and claws.
Where did they go?

FOREBODING

I could not call Ravenette's

Seeing another

Person cheating.

We had never really

Been together.

We were never really

Into the mind thing.

We never did much talking.

But, at our last encounter,

A sixth sense suddenly struck me.

It was the walking death she'd been with.

Sleep with one person and

You sleep with all of that lover's lovers.

That was the message.

That was it, I had to warn her.

Message delivered.

The blank, pale stare said it all.

An angel lost her teeth, claws, and wings.

HOSPITAL STAY

While Ravenette slept
Her life seemed lifeless
While the sun through panes
Of glass imposed its will.

So many Nights
Had wept
Their raindrops on
Her window sill.

Upon the streets,
A hustle and a bustle,
Eyeless to the fallen star
That lay upon a bed of nails.

The barks of dogs,
The purrs of cats,
Against the death throes
Of a nightingale.

Flap you angels, flap your wings,
For oh,
Oh,
Oh,
In my heart,
How my Ravenette sings.
How my Ravenette clings.

LETTER TO AN ANGEL

Dear Master Angel,

Ravenette has cried,
And cried enough.
Take her under wing
Tomorrow morning.
She will be free,
But mine tonight,
And will be yours
When Earth is dawning.

I'll hold her hand,
And kiss her brow,
And give her one
last sweet embrace.
Her memory wipe
Of all regrets,
And if mine hurts,
Remove my face.

P.S.

Don't tell her
I refused her plea.
I'll carry both
Our pains with me.

GRAVE GOODBYE

A score is far too young for graves.
Four score is what the minimum should be.
Ravenette could have lived to be a hundred.

What a merciful God, to have given us disease,
To destroy His own angels.

I wondered what the other angels thought
About the human image.

Did we merely *look* like God?
Seemed that is where the similarities ended.

All Ravenette wanted was
To love and be loved.

I think that is more God-like.
However, it was too late.
The lid had closed on God.

JAMEENA

JAMEENA'S EXOTIC DANCE

The Ocean undulates upon the stage,

Without the moon,

Or benefit of sun.

Yet, stars dance on her never tiring age,

And sun is brought to those whose day is done.

No promises ensue with those who dream

Of bathing in her crashing tides of sin,

But minds do wander,

For a ray or beam,

To keep their rushing rivers rushing in.

The wavelets call the sailors out to sea,

Where some may grasp the beauty of her waves;

But most will stand on dry reality,

Content or discontent,

With land for graves.

To drown in Ocean's depths,

Uncleansed, one goes, for there

Is where her dirty water flows.

THE LURE

Jameena

    Reggae in ebony

Statuesque goddess

    Five-ten in six-inch heels

Seeking attention

    Demanding attention

        Getting attention

Dark chocolate thighs opening and closing

Revealing an opposing white G-string

Underneath the G is the promise of sex

        Seeking attention

    Demanding attention

Getting attention

            Someone gets her attention

He puts the bill in her string

Probably swearing he has reeled her in

Then the line snaps

And her lure moves on to catch another fish.

A FACE IN THE CROWD

Jameena noticed me and took a liking.

Hell if I knew why if it wasn't for money.

She rubbed my thigh

The moment she sat next to me.

Part of the act.

I knew she knew I wanted her.

Everybody in the strip joint wanted her.

Something to do with

What my dad once told me:

    Some women belong to everyone.

I stared at her face to find out if it was true.

Was she for everyone?

I searched but no answer.

Her panther-like eyes did not reveal a thing either.

But a hunger.

Finally the goddess spoke,
>	I think you're a nice guy.
Really, how's that?

I've danced a string away from naked
And here I sit the same and you've done
Nothing but stare at my face.

I agreed with her and we talked, while I tried to
Figure out to what group of stars her eyes belonged.

IN A FAR AWAY PLACE

The young studs were boisterous
As they watched Jameena's
Half-clothed perfect body
Ripple across the stage.
The light gauze peeled slowly off her body
Promised nothing short of mayhem in the groin,
And yet, promised nothing—but the view.
She was a storm, looking better all the time,
Her swaying a cause for jealousy among the
Palm trees of Jamaica or any other island.

Upon her neck of ebony silk
Black, shiny curls bounteously fell,
And the liquor-laden loud-mouths
Tossed bills at her feet,
And held fists full of dollars
To bring her to them.
Had they really bothered to look
Into her eyes, she was never onstage.

THE RAPE OF JAMEENA

A strong woman could probably

Beat a strong man, but not likely two or three.

And all because she wouldn't give herself, they took her.

She carried a knife, just didn't get a chance to use it.

Otherwise, I think she would've killed them.

I helped her off the stoop,

Gave her a ride home, (she did not want the cops)

Stayed a bit, because she said she needed a nice guy around.

She took a long time in the shower,

Scrubbing her soul paper-thin.

And when she was ready,

She cried in my arms the rest of the night.

I told her I was not like that.

She said she would've stabbed me in the

Heart if she thought I was.

CAFÉ AU LAIT

I guess what I

wanted was

to hear Jameena say

I'll give up the strip joint for you.

I'll always be with you.

I'll love no one but you.

I can't live without you.

I am the coffee and you the milk.

We'll live on love.

WAKE UP!

My rent is past due,

And you can't afford me.

(Ah, how I was young and foolish like I was supposed to be)

SWEET CHOCOLATE

Jameena spent the night with me
                                      getting spent
Until finally sleep overwhelmed her

I touched her gently on the shoulder
And then went about my business of insomnia
thinking
                how I loved sweet dark chocolate
How the heat of one's fingers makes it smooth
The creamy texture of it teasing the tongue
Perverse flavor
Melted chocolate
            So good for the libido
Most of all—being swallowed by chocolate
(who eats whom?)
Suddenly I felt the urge to caress Jameena
And while I did, I took a taste of her, and she stirred.
Mmmmmm.
Decadent!

BLENDING IN

Jameena's reggae music in the background
      My bolero music in the foreground
On her table:
curry goat, fried dumplings, spicy patties,
callaloo fritters, rice and peas,
fried soft plaintain, fried pork chops,
baked chicken, salad, bread,
Lignum Vitae adorned napkins . . .
      On my table:
      arroz con gandules, pernil, bacalaitos,
      rice and beans, fried hard plaintain,
      oven-baked pork chops,
      fried chicken, salad, bread,
      Flor de Maga adorned napkins . . .
Appleton Rum for Jameena, Bacardi Rum for me.
A good woman and a nice guy, in one bed,
And suddenly, there we were—
      JamRicanizing.
Making love unifies everyone.

ONSTAGE LOOKING OUT

People with money think
    they own people without.

Was Jameena's body worth the dollar?   Jameena was priceless,
      And that strip-dollar was an insult.

I was going to stop myself
      from insulting.
      I wanted her to stop, and wished
      Everyone would too.

However, it was twisted.
To stop the insult was to be insulting.

I think I insulted Jameena,

        And all the other girls who danced there.

I forgot to look at the other side of the coin.

I was tampering with their livelihood.

I realized, from the vantage point of the stage,

Every forehead looking up

Had a dollar sign stamped on it,

Including my own.

In the end,

My dollar sign was speaking louder than I was.

CHICAGO BOUND

Without warning Jameena was gone.

Stay away too long and you may
Find people have disappeared.

Stay away too long and you may find
People have forgotten you.

Then again, you may find both have occurred.

That's reality.
Nothing to do with sex.
Or love.

Which is it about absence?
(Fonder or out of mind)
It seems Love always stays put, like a tree,
And it is we who come and go
Beneath its branches.

AKSHARANI

UNEXPECTED GUEST

I was an unexpected guest.

I merely saw an old man slowly walking

Alongside the road, and offered

To give him a lift home.

He spoke little English

But he made it clear

He could not permit me to

Leave his home without offering me

Something in return.

I asked for water,

While his daughter,

Aksharani, thanked me for my kindness.

Politeness required conversation,

And the freedom to indulge it.

To Aksharani, freedom in America

Was of no consequence,

Since her family from Mumbai

Had cultivated tradition in her heart,

And it was her way.

Tradition follows its own footsteps

No matter where it travels,

Even when it makes its first impressions

For others to step into.

My dad taught me that.

Her dad taught her that.

Then Aksharani said I must have

More than just water,

And produced a tray from the kitchen.

Her dad was all smiles, while

We had chocolate chip cookies with milk,

While Aksharani made delicious sounds,

And I was pleased that sharing brought

About such peace and happiness.

I wondered if the United Nations liked

Chocolate chip cookies and milk.

EXOTICNESS

Aksharani was from the land

Of the Kama Sutra,

Written by Vātsyāyana

In a time when women

Were not permitted to read.

In the event of the absence of men,

How then would the sacred

Lotus flower know

What was written?

Gazing at Aksharani,

A mysterious creation of exoticness,

A woman of India would not need

To read the Kama Sutra,

Being one the cause of such inspiration.

SATISFYING HUNGER

I ask you Aksharani:
How do you do the honorable thing
Being of two different worlds,
When doing so means remaining
Two worlds apart?
Which speaks louder, tradition or love?
Which one will you save in your heart
If you can only save one?

To falter is to disgrace both families.
Your disgrace more so, to risk being
Shunned like a plague.

Then again, there is the taboo,
The secret tryst, to satisfy a certain hunger.
So, Aksharani, lotus princess, for now,
On your hidden plate,
Let me be the fish you devour completely.

PARADISE

I said to Aksharani:

> Love is love.
> One should seek it
> With one's eyes closed.
> Once one finds love,
> If one opens one's eyes
> And is disappointed,
> Then one sought love
> With the mind and not the heart.
> If one opens one's eyes
> And remains genuinely afire,
> In the heart, eyes, and mind,
> Then one has found love.
> The fire in the loins will follow naturally.
> If one is afire only in the loins,
> Then one has found lust not love.

Aksharani replied:

> Love is the closest thing to
> Paradise we have.
>
> Sometimes, to find paradise, we must first
> Get the lust out of the way.
>
> Furthermore, men do not have
> A monopoly on lust.

REPARTEE

Aksharani said to me:

Yesterday I dreamt I was

Standing in the middle of a field

That longed for the Bajra

To be planted when the season is right.

It needed a Raja to plant the seeds.

I am like that field.

I replied:

Today I dream by day,

For last night I could not sleep

Thinking myself a Raja

Resting upon your field

After the seeds were planted.

FOR A PINK LOTUS

I said to Aksharani:

Above the mud the Pink Lotus grows,

The supreme lotus,

To catch the eye

Of the highest deity, *Ganesha*,

The elephant-deity who rides a mouse.

Should *Shiva*, death and destroyer, be worried

His eye will not catch you?

If *Krishna*, the blue-skinned deity,

Is closest to the heart of the masses,

How close is he to your heart?

Will *Rama* tell the truth and say you are above him?

Speaking of truth, will the Sustainer of Life, *Vishnu*,

In all his righteousness preserve your beauty?

Will your pink petals soothe the breast of the
Mighty ape, *Hanuman,* and delay him from
His expedition against evil forces?

Will *Lakshmi* keep you
In your household forever?

Will *Durga* make you as
inaccessible as herself?

Kali has her protruding tongue, eyes of red,
And blood upon her breasts.
Does she compare her breasts to yours?

If *Saraswati* gives you her knowledge,
What would you do with it?

In the end, for all their powers,

The greatest power is love.

Be that, the goddess of love.

Be yourself,

And you will be the most powerful.

THE NOISELESS DEITY

I said to Aksharani:

God makes no noise
For it is the nature of God.
I have never met Him in church,
And I don't think I will find Him
In the temples of any Hindu god.

However, there is a higher power
I feel when I rest upon your breasts.
There is a fire from your flesh
Only a god could have created.
There is a beauty upon your face that is divine.

When you breathe, it transforms into a storm.
And when we make love, God remains most quiet,
So we can hear each other's heartbeat,
And know He is there; He is silent, because
He wants *us* to make all the noise.

THE ARROW OF LOVE

Hear me, Aksharani:

I begged let loose the sharp arrows
Of my Cupid and your Ram
To strike the heart of who you are
And who I am.

The pain we feel has bared no wound,
For no flesh is broken.
And there's no ointment to rub
On words we may have spoken.

Of Tradition and of Love,
We've asked before:
Which will rule the heart forevermore?

I'll ask Aphrodite,
You ask Kama the same.

For when it comes to broken hearts,
They each must share the blame.

ONE FOR TRADITION

I contemplated with Aksharani:

We have our stories
We have our beliefs
We inherited our ways of life
We have our lands
We have our homes

In your home you were plain.
In my home I was plain.
In my home you were exotic.
In your home I was exotic.

We lovingly lusted and lusted for love
And loved for love and loved lovingly

Under what rubric then
Will we place what we had?

Let us say we shared a

Chocolate chip cookie and
A glass of milk
And be happy we did.

Now, let us put it under the rubric of *Living*.

AN INDIAN WEDDING

I imagined Aksharani bathing after the
Rubbing of turmeric paste all over her body.

I imagined her glowing from
Head to toe from the Haldi makeup.

I imagined her hands covered in an exotic
Brown design as the Mehndi ritual requires.

Special stress given to red lip color
And the red bindi on her forehead,
Adorned with white beautiful decorations.

Then the enveloping of her body
In a colorful and luxurious wedding attire.

All of this made me wonder:
How do you make Beauty
More beautiful in the first place?

You do not.
You cannot.
Still, we gift wrap precious jewels.

YU-SEONG

THE INTRODUCTION

Yu-seong,
Flower of Busan,
I missed you.

I didn't know this
Until I met you.

How did Fate and Time
Keep us apart for so long?

You came gift wrapped,
In your black, flared,
Twist-knit mini-skirt,
With the white blouse,
Black-ribboned, ruffled neck.
Your skin of alabaster to match.
While underneath I could tell,
By falling into your eyes, your soul
Burned like the red chili pepper
One uses to make kimchi.

And, of course,
The surprise you brought me.
The ego to match the red chili pepper.
The gift of being you.

MOON IN THE FLESH

You are Yu-seong, silver moon rising,
Bright in all your beauty
Enthralling me with your sorcery
Till my soul howls.

Your moonbeams descend
From the being of my lady,
Engaging me with your gaze
Till my soul howls.

Moon in silver exultation,
You are the arresting one
Who constantly tortures me
Till I howl at you like a wolf.

NO SHAME

Yu-seong, you begged me to leave you alone.
You begged me not to send you flowers.
You begged me not to stuff you with kimchi.
You begged me not to make you drunk with Soju.
You begged me not to trespass onto your orchard.
You begged me to stay out of sight.

Then you took me out of your box of toys
And let your fiery loins punish me.
You carved you had *no shame* in red upon my back
With the aroused claws of your demon dragon.
And you were pleased I did as you asked.

SELFISH

It is hard to see myself in a house
Of mirrors when you are there intensified.

No matter where I stand,
I am behind you and cannot
See myself at all.

Then you look again, increased.
It is the only place you look.

When you look into your own eyes,
Do you see yourself there as well
Redoubled exponentially?

You ask do I worship you.
You ask what love is.

Yes, Yu-seong, I am well aware
Just because you need me doesn't
Mean at all you love me.

At least your body aches for me.
That I can see without duplicitous mirrors.

DAYS OF BLUE

Your absence, Yu-seong, makes me blue.

The blue of the sky and mine are different—
I know for whom I long for, the sky does not.

If you were summer green,
And the somber autumn
Killed you with its hues,
Autumn did not know you.

If the white snow fell,
And you do not return pink in the spring,
The cold winter did not know you.

I am blue because
I know for whom I long for.
I have sighed your name
To the seasons and the sky.

FOOLISHNESS

Your indulgences, Yu-seong, deserve caution.
You consider yourself atop the highest mountain,
But below you are the clouds of living rain.

Stay at that height—
And you will miss the streams,
And you will miss the lakes,
And you will miss the oceans,
And you will miss the mud.

The Mugunghwa will grow without you.
Others will get the Tulips and Red Roses.

Come down and rest with me
Under my umbrella, before you tumble,
And let us wait for the sun together.

PETALS

Yu-seong, do not blame
The wind for the falling petals.

Those petals are memories,
Precious on the mind.

Years from now, when we are old,
They will be all we have,
When we can have no more.

They will carry us,
When our limbs give way.

They will breathe for us
When we can barely breathe.

They will love us
When we can no longer love.

You are to blame, not the wind.
You have confirmed it
With the tornado from your heart.

YET ANOTHER FLEETING MOMENT

Yu-seong, you returned in the night,
Barging in on me,
And wantonly stretched
Yourself across my bed.

The dark room gave in and
The universe lit up, and
Winds howled outside my window
Like voices from heaven.

But I felt my love above the bed
Peering down on us.

Outside, an unyielding dog bayed
In the darkness
Throughout your physical irruption
And beyond.

The dog in the darkness begged.
(Let Yu-seong go! Let Yu-seong her go!)

Hush, dog.
I will run with the pack soon enough.

AN UNDERSTANDING

Yu-seong, why kept it you a secret?

If honor bids you hurry homeland,
It is an honor to obey.

Morning comes too soon now,
Let us give this night what still remains,
For in our youth our youthful
Bodies must be spent.

Then let us name a star our love.
I'll name one for this poem.

Writing a poem of my love for you is easy.
 Not loving it with you will be hard.

NOT IN THE STARS

Yu-seong,
Despite how fate has seen it fit,
For now let's melt in sweet embrace,
And kiss,
A kiss,
A lasting kiss,
Then let me gaze upon your face,
So I may paint my mind with you,
Your face, your eyes, your lips,
And silken hair,
Until your image,
Etched upon my heart and soul,
Forever keeps you there.

For love will ever keep you there.

BAYBEE

BODACIOUS BAYBEE

Baybee,
Were it you were ugly, and I still on fire,
Despite your fashion faux-pas, or glamor less,
A shrinking violet, a total mess,

In fact, so plain, in face or old attire,
Where still it would climb my passion higher,
Then I'll have fallen for a genuine delight,
Which has nothing at all to do with sight.

If that were the case,
I'd take a bow,
But me outrageous!
You bodacious!
Your beautiful face and body
Will do

And how!

NO VENUS

Baybee, oh Baybee,
I don't need
A Venus for my love.

All pedestals are clouds,
And Icarus knew late the heavy humor
Of a man, far above this fragile world,
Where fluid wings tempt fate.

On this earthly soil for you I wait,
Where passion's eyes entreat the lips
To meet in whispered songs of mortal love
That wake the nature of the flesh,
So frail—and sweet!

And we will dance
Above the gods
Beneath your feet.

I DON'T BLAME THE WIND

Your blouse is unbuttoned.
You flaunt your silk skirt, with sash untied,
And stand before the window,
Your hair a dreadful mess,
No makeup at all, pale from drinking
Too much at the party.

Your eructations and other gases
Are just not lady like, especially
When you open up the window
And the wind badly blows my way.

You bring your hands up to put
Your hair up in a bun, and your
Feeble coverings try to flap away
From your malodorous underarms
And dried body perspirations
Of the night before.

Then, I look at your beautifully exposed body,
And Baybee, I don't blame the wind,
Because I'm the one who loved
You up last night.

SAVAGE LOVE

A man,
When walking down the streets,
Wants a lady on his arm,
A lady of attraction.

In bed, between the sheets,
He wants a lady of the evening,
One who can appreciate a romp
And share the satisfaction.

But damn, Baybee, you're killing me!
Let's walk awhile, woman!

STRING HAIKU FOR MY BAYBEE

your hair in a bun
a body tight as a spring
so my spring is sprung

body like the spring
a lust as hot as pepper
sexy tinkering

hot chili pepper
Kama Sutra positions
my jungle leopard

every position
satisfaction guaranteed
flowery vision

my love guaranteed
watching you sleep after sex
basking in the need

you sleep after sex
I've given you my whole world
don't remove the hex

TAKE YOUR TIME

Every time we're going out, Baybee,
You linger in the shower.
The bar of soap, of apricot scent,
Slides up and down your body,
Creating tingly bubbles; the shampoo and
Conditioner must create voluminous
Hair; and your little lady must be
Dried and powdered just right.

You're in no rush.
You linger in the dressing room.
The Victoria's Secret unmentionables
Must be carefully placed and snug.
The Frederick's of Hollywood stockings
You slide slowly up your smoothly shaved
Legs, with such ritualistic finesse,
Were made just for you.

You linger at your mirror until
You know you are a goddess,
A goddess worth the wait.

It makes a man like me proud to be a man.
I was dressed and ready in ten minutes.

BRIEF ENCOUNTER

From the span that is your life, Baybee,
 Give me a while, no matter its brevity.
Forget about all that has gone before
Forget all about what will come after this
So you and I can make a perfect present.

When it comes to passion, we must not waste
Our endowments, thoughts, feelings and sense,
But instead, let us bask in our insanity.
Buried in your moment, I falling into it.

There is no past, there is no future,
There is only now, the flatness of our bodies,
The burn, the embrace, the closing of our eyes,
Which all began the moment our lips met!
This is it.
Let us live it, this very moment.
Stopping time right
Here.

THE BED

So decadent, Baybee, the ways of sin.
Yet is it really sin at all
If in concordance we give in
And nary an eye has seen us fall?

The little death, once all is done,
Intertwined across the bed
We are like statues, but still, it goes on
Inside my head.

FLOWERS BLOOM

Is there *really*
A god that says it is so?

A momma runs towards
Her crying baby's call.

Do you *really* need
A god to say it is so.

I need you, you need me,
That's all.

We don't *really* need a god
To tell us it is so.

Flowers bloom, Baybee,
And flowers fall.

That's all.

METEORIC

Oh, Baybee,
Love did we not so brilliantly?

Comets envied us our
Spectacular journey.

Dwarfed their tails
We did, headlong
Towards the stars.

The Earth and the Moon
Arrived in a blink of an eye.

We were unstoppable!

Yet,
You crashed into the Earth,
I, pummeled the Moon.

Still, let us make a pact.
Every now and then,
Let us look into each other's eyes
And say
I was there.

ESPERANZA

HOPE

The name *Esperanza* means *Hope*.

She consists of only one poem,
The one which, even when shattered,
Still stands before you.

She is invincible,
Even when she has been destroyed.

You may not see her,
Still, she is there.

She is someone you
Should never give up.

She is someone
You should never allow
To be taken from you.
She breathes life.

Life and Hope
Are always deeply
In love with each other.

She is my best muse.
The promise of a love to come.

THE END

About the Author

The author started writing poetry in High School where he was first introduced to the works of Shakespeare, Edgar Allen Poe, and Edna St. Vincent Millay, his three favorite poets.

He also has his own poetry website:

www.poeticon.com

Other books by the author:

A Reason for Rhyme

The Suicide Sonnets

Count Edweird Lefang's Rhymin' Halloween

A Candle on Fire

Poems for Edna

The Burning of Bishop Nicholas Ridley

www.ingramcontent.com/pod-product-compliance
Lightning Source LLC
LaVergne TN
LVHW051838080426
835512LV00018B/2939